BRIEF MEDITATIONS WHEN THE CHURCH IS GATHERED AROUND THE LORD'S TABLE

by
Gary G. Jenkins
Christian Minister

Foreword

The average Communion Meditation is between 2 1/2 and 5 minutes long, with a few notable exceptions that could be easily mistaken for the sermon. While it is this writer's opinion that the Lord's Supper is the "highlight" of our Worship Service, I do not believe that requires a lengthy Communion Meditation from elder or preacher. The focus should be on the "partaking" and the silent communing with our Lord and Saviour.

Most of these meditations should be shared in no more than 60 seconds. This does several things. (a) It enables the one charged with this responsibility to memorize without great difficulty what will be said. It can then be shared without obviously reading the material. (b) It suggests a thought, but leaves the greater burden of participation upon each individual Christian. The Lord's Table is indeed then the center of our attention.

These brief Communion Meditations are shared in the hope that they can meet a need and direct our attention afresh to "Jesus Christ — bleeding — upon the earth He made." By His blood our sins are covered. A testimony until He comes again".

In Christ's service,

Gary G. Jenkins

FOR FRIEND AND FOE

(1) "For I received from the Lord that which I also delivered to you, that the Lord Jesus in the night in which He was betrayed took bread" (I Cor. 11:23, RSV). The Scripture records that He took bread and broke it — the same night He was betrayed. Amazing, isn't it! He was giving Himself not only for Peter, Andrew, James and John — but also for Judas! Not just for that handful of almost perfect few who live around us. But also for ME ... imperfect though I am... and you!

REDEDICATION

(2) This is the best time for Christians to rededicate themselves. Each one of us, in these silent moments before we hold the cup and bread, needs to take stock of our lives. We each know we should do ... could do better, but we must ask now for His help and forgiveness. "Wash me, and I shall be whiter than snow." What tremendous burdens are lifted by that thought.

WHAT DIFFERENCE?

(3) What difference does a bit of bread and a swallow of grape juice make? No one can say what they can mean for you — except you! It is, remember, in the "remembering" that the blessing comes. His Body — broken! His blood — shed! For You and Me!

GOOD AND BAD

(4) There are good and bad memories. Good ones of days gone past when things seemed cleaner—clearer—quieter—friendlier. Experiences that enriched our lives. Bad memories that haunt us in dreams or at least our thought. Memories we wish we could erase.

"Do this in Remembrance of Me." It's both good and bad. Good, because He loved us enough to die for our sins; Bad, because it cost Him such a price for our salvation!

NO LORD'S SUPPER

(5) Friends, while on vacation, related their disappointment when traveling and worshipping in a strange church that they did not observe the Lord's Supper. They said that it just did not "seem right" to them.

I thought — isn't it strange how some people see this as just a meaningless ritual that makes the service last an extra 5-10 minutes, while others have grown to love and deeply appreciate this quiet time in the worship service.

It begins on the day of our baptism — accepting Jesus as Lord and Saviour and continues on through the years so that some people make special plans to be where they can worship and "break bread" — remembering the sacrifice of Christ.

It's just not the same — without it!

LIFE'S PERSPECTIVE

(6) A man called from the airport as he traveled through on business. We talked. During the conversation he said that his high speed travel had upset his idea of time.

Life can do that to all of us. It eats away at our perspective. This brief time at the Lord's Table can help us all get our lives back into God's perspective.

HALLOWED GROUND

(7) William Cowper wrote:
> "Jesus, where'er Thy people meet,
> There they behold Thy mercy-seat;
> Where'er they seek Thee, Thou art found,
> And every place is hallowed ground."

It is not the burning bush, the church building, or this table that are Holy. It is the presence of God at these places that makes them so very important to us.

HOW OFTEN?

(8) When reading in a denominational magazine, this question was raised: "How often should we celebrate the Lord's Supper?" The writer didn't really answer the question, but rather referred to their particular Denominational Book which required it at least once a quarter. Someone might inquire further, "But what does the Bible teach?"

We remember the Lord's death —— His loving sacrifice for us. I wonder how He feels when His children find it too much trouble for us to remember this, but once a quarter??

Of course, it is surely as bad, if we serve it each week but then His children don't make the effort to come about his table.

REVEAL THY PRESENCE

(9) Reveal Thy presence now, O Lord,
     As in the Upper Room of old;
     Break Thou our bread, grace Thou our board,
     And keep our hearts from growing cold.

Thomas Tiplady, 1882-1967

BLESSING AND OBEDIENCE

(10) A group of Christians were talking about the fact that we seem to go through cycles of appreciation for the Lord's Supper. We really receive a blessing one time — another time it is just habit.

Besides what we receive from this time with our Lord, is there not another dimension that we often forget. Jesus said "Take this and share it among yourselves" (Luke 22:17, NASV). It is a request that speaks of obedience and makes no promise as to how we shall feel while doing it. When we read in Acts of the Church of the First Century we see that they did this each Sunday not for their pleasure but in humble obedience to their Saviour's request. In obedience — we now remember!

"OUTWITTED"

(11) "He drew a circle that shut me out —
Heretic, rebel, a thing to flout.
But Love and I had the wit to win.
We drew a circle that took him in!"

Edwin Markham

The poet talks about hate and love. Just when Christ was most cruelly tested, He conquered — by loving us all the more!

NO EGO PROBLEM

(12) Jesus doesn't have a supreme ego that needs to be fed by our weekly gathering about His table, but we need it ... lest we get life out of perspective. Who we are. How we came to have this life that we now enjoy as Christians. It is... important for us!

SIN NO MORE

(13) "Sin no more." Thus Jesus spoke to the sick man by the pool of Bethesda, whom he had healed (John 5.14). The same command He gave to the woman that was found in adultery (John 8:11). Jesus says the same to every one of us whom He has shown mercy to, whose sickness He has healed, and whose life He has redeemed from destruction. Thus He speaks to everyone who goes forth from this important feast: "Go hence; sin no more."

NOT ME!

(14) After Jesus and His disciples had shared that last special meal together, they went out to the Mount of Olives. It was there that Jesus foretold of His disciples falling away from Him. Peter's response was "Even though all fall away, yet I will not" (Mark 14:29, NASV). We all remember the result of Peter's brag.

We all make boasts to God that we sometimes fail to live up to. This is a time to be truly humble as we think of His love to our unworthy selves.

NONSENSE

(15) Some object that Communion every Sunday makes it lose its sacredness and influence in our lives.

This deals with human weakness, but if always true it would logically follow a person should pray but once a month or hear a sermon but twice a year to receive their full impact. These folks should be more religious than those who pray daily.

Is a Mother's love less appreciated because it is experienced every day rather than once a month or once a year? Nonsense!

BODY AND SIN — BROKEN

(16) Luke 22:19 records that Jesus took bread and gave thanks for it.   He then broke it and gave it to the disciples saying, "This is my body, given for you."

Just what was about to happen? Sin in the hearts of men — ripped Jesus Christ. A healer. A lover of the poor and rich. One who cared for little children, Sin broke Him away from the world, but in that terrible miscarriage of justice — life won an amazing reversal over death.

His body was broken and with it, the grip of sin over our lives was also broken. This is a part of the meaning of the Lord's Supper.

DEEP AND WIDE

(17) We sing that little chorus before we can understand it completely and some grow up never understanding. "Deep and Wide! Deep and Wide! There is a fountain, flowing deep and wide!"

Yes, there is a fountain and no matter how far apart we might stretch our arms, they cannot describe its dimensions. "Deep" enough to cover a multitude of sins. "Wide" enough to reach to everyone — no matter how far away they have strayed.

THE CHOICE

(18) Dorothy L. Sayers, in a play, "The Choice of the Cross" — writes these words.

"Hard it is, very hard,
To travel up the slow and stoney road
To Calvary to redeem mankind; for better
To make but one resplendent miracle,
Lean through the cloud,

lift the right hand of power
And with a sudden lightning —
smite the world perfect.
Yet this was not God's way, Who had the power,
But set it by, choosing the cross, the thorn,
The sorrowful wounds,
something there is, perhaps
That power destroys in passing,
something supreme,
To whose great value in the eyes of God
That cross, that thorn,
and those five wounds bear witness."

STILL GROWING

(19) One men said, "Here I am 58 years old and I still don't know what I'm going to do when I grow up."

Each of us is still growing. We make many mistakes — and sometimes we do a few things right. No one should ever fail to approach this table because they feel "unfit."

The Scriptures (I Cor. 11:27) caution about partaking in an "unworthy manner". It means in a silly manner rather than with serious consideration. Our unfitness is the very reason this time with Christ is so important to Christians. None of us — is fully grown in Christ yet!

ACCEPTED WITHOUT BRIBES

(20) A man told of coming home one evening and finding the neighborhood children surrounding a little

girl that they usually ignored. She was a lonely little girl most of the time, but on closer examination of the group he could see that she had given each child a popsicle. This was the reason for her new-found popularity. She had built a bridge of friendship through a gift. It is sad to see a child that must offer a fistful of candy for acceptance.

You and I are "accepted" without popsicles and candy — even with our Sins. The Lord's Supper reminds the Christian, "You have been forgiven! You are accepted!"

BOUGHT WITH A PRICE

(21) Have you ever wondered why Christ had to suffer so for us? Wondered why He could not have somehow taken away our sins in a less painful way — perhaps even enjoying it. Yes, I suppose He could — but God is wiser.

Suffering brings people closer together like nothing else. We could easily forget His joy and pleasure. We cannot forget His suffering! "...You are not your own... for you have been bought with a price..." (I Cor. 6:20, NASV).

AMAZING!

(22) "While we were yet helpless at the right time Christ died for the ungodly. Why, one will hardly die for a righteous man — though perhaps for a good man one will dare even to die. But God shows His love for us in

that while we were yet sinners Christ died for us" (Romans 5:6-8, KJV).

Unbelievable! Amazing! But True!

HIS TABLE

(23) We prepare the Communion emblems — but it was Christ who instituted it. He invited to this table. We can only accept it or reject it for ourselves alone. That is our only choice. This is His table — open to all believers in Christ as He would invite them.

DO YOU THIRST?

(24) Jesus cried out, "I thirst" (John 19:28), from upon the cross. Those were human words and we imagine that we know what He meant, — but do we?

When we come here — to this table, do we have a thirst of the soul that cries out? This is His blood, shed, that the dry, ugliness of our lives might be moistened, softened, cleansed — forgiven!

WOUNDED BECAUSE OF US

(25) "Surely He has borne our griefs and carried our sorrows, yet we esteemed Him stricken, smitten by God, and afflicted. But He was wounded for our transgressions, He was bruised for our iniquities; upon Him was the chastisement that made us whole, and with His stripes we are healed. All we like sheep have gone

astray; we have turned every one to his own way..."
(Isaiah 53:4-6, KJV).

"...All have sinned and fallen short of the glory of
God" (Rom. 3:23, NASV).

"TAKE AND EAT"

(26) And when He had given thanks He took
bread and broke it and said "Take and eat". He gave
part of the loaf to John, who broke a piece from it and
passed it to James. And James broke a chunk from it
and passed it to Peter, who tore a piece from it and
passed it to Matthew. When Matthew had his portion, he
passed it on. So it was that the loaf passed from hand
to hand until each man had a part. Then they ate
together and were fed.

When we come to this time of the Lord's Supper,
we reenact the drama of the early Christian Church.
Its elements are simple but their meaning is profound.
Its gestures are gentle but their significance is great.
We place bread on the table; we pass it on to one
another; we take it and eat — much as the first
Christians did.

MY GLORY—THE CROSS

(27) "I take, O Cross, thy shadow
　　　For my abiding-place;
　　　I ask no other sunshine than
　　　The sunshine of His face;
　　　Content to let the world go by,
　　　To know no gain nor loss

My sinful self my only shame,
My glory all, the Cross."
                    Elizabeth C. Clephane (1830-1869)

BOTH SHARED AND PERSONAL

(28) The church — the Body of Christ — is a collection of individual members. It is both individual and a collective group. WE are part of THEY. We should not expect others to do what we won't do. Yet we are judged by God. As individuals. What others do — good or bad — is not held against us.

During the Communion service, we share an important moment with other "Believers," but it is also a unique moment that is personal. Just between God and each of us!

THE LOVE OF GOD

(29) We talk a lot about the love of God through Christ Jesus His Son. We also sing about it — but at this table — we remember again (silently this time) in our mind's eye, the action that demonstrated that love.

Has anyone else ever died — for you?

A TIME OF JOY

(30) As we gather about this table, it is a time of joy also. Joy — because from Christ's death comes the power to forgive our sin and from that comes the hope, the promise of eternal life.

Someone has said, "A Christian ought to smile —
Christ may come tonight! A non-Christian ought to smile
— because Christ didn't come last night!"

JUST LIKE THE EARLY CHURCH

(31) Acts 2:42 is very clear about the activities of
the early church. "They continued steadily learning the
teachings of the apostles, and joined in their fellowship,
in the breaking of bread, and in prayer." We also are
involved in these things here today. Their meal included
the grateful remembering of their Lord's death.
Likewise, with thankfulness in our hearts, we pause to
remember His body — broken; his blood — shed.

FOR THE WORST OF TIME

(32) Part of the Communion service is a reference
to the time and the situation. "On the night that he was
betrayed took bread" (I Cor. 11:23) is what the
scriptures say.

It seems that here is a real insight into the nature
of our faith. Our faith is at its best not in some quiet
and simple setting but it shines best in the midst of
temptations, betrayal, and denial. Not for the best of
times — but the worst.

"NOT OURS"

(33) For a period of years we worshipped in a
rented school building until we could build our own.
When we came to the Communion service we gathered

about an old scarred desk. The fact that it was not "our table" carried new significance. What was shared and what it stands for was what made it important. It was for all those who are bound to Christ by his sacrifice on Calvary.

THEY RECOGNIZED HIM

(34) Luke tells of two disciples walking on the road to Emmaus after Jesus' death. They were still not sure of His resurrection. A stranger walked with them and then stayed with them when they invited Him. Then when they ate supper the Scripture says..."He was recognized by them in the breaking of the bread" (Luke 24:35, NASV). We still can recognize Him at this table.

WHY?

(35) "And while they were eating, Jesus took some bread, and after a blessing, He broke it and gave it to the disciples, and said, "Take, eat: this is my body" (Matt. 26:26-29, NASV). And He took a cup and gave thanks and gave it to them, saying, "Drink from it, all of you; for this is my blood of the covenant which is to be shed on behalf of many for forgiveness of sins. But I say to you, I will not drink of the fruit of the vine from now on until that day when I drink it new with you in My Father's kingdom."

Why do we drink this cup? Why do we eat this bread? Because He commanded it — in remembrance of Him.

Not because others do...

Not because there is any special magic in it...
But because we love our Lord
and desire to remember Him
as often as we meet.

MY JESUS, I LOVE THEE

(36) We sing, "My Jesus, I Love Thee." It's easy to sing those words, easy to say them. But it is when we see that visual image of Jesus hanging in blood-caked pain — Loving us ... that is when we really measure our love. It is not an easy matter to dismiss.

PILGRIM'S PROGRESS

(37) John Bunyan, in The Pilgrim's Progress, tells how, when the pilgrim with his burden arrived at the cross, and looked by faith to the Saviour, his burden of sin fell off and was buried in the grave. He then exclaimed:

> "Blest cross! Blest sepulcher! Blest rather be,
> the man that there was put to shame for me!"

HYPOCRITES

(38) We all know people who don't attend church because they say, "Those people are a bunch of hypocrites". A good response might be, "Yes, the church is full of hypocrites, but there is always room for one more: why don't you come?"

We are all phony, in differing degrees. The Lord's Supper is good for us. It's quiet — no brag or show, just between you and God. He knows us, so there is no need for pretence. It's one thing that helps to keep us hypocrites humble.

ONE ON ONE

(39) Jesus chose 12 Apostles —— not 12,000. He chose them one by one. It seems He made some personal contact with each one before calling him. Today we have many churches. Some of them quite large. Preaching and teaching to thousands. One can feel lost in the crowd.

Still I'm convinced that Christ still has the capacity and desire to know us each personally as individuals. This quiet time of communion may very well be one of the important times that He uses to get to know us.

THOSE ABSENT

(40) As we gather about this Holy Table we should be aware of those who are absent. Those who might have been at the Lord's Table if we had been more faithful in our evangelistic responsibility. There is an evangelistic message in the Lord's Supper which no Christian should overlook. "For the Son of Man came to seek and to save the lost" (Luke 19:10). The same concern for the lost that was in our Saviour's heart should be in ours also.

TOO OFTEN

(41) "For I received from the Lord that which I also delivered to you, that the Lord Jesus in the night in which He was betrayed took bread; and when He had given thanks, He broke it, and said, 'This is my body, which is for you; do this in remembrance of me.' In the same way He took the cup also, after supper, saying, 'This cup is the new covenant in My blood; do this, as often as you drink it, in remembrance of Me.' For as often as you eat this bread and drink the cup, you proclaim the Lord's death until He comes" (I Cor. 11:23-26, NASV).

"Do this in remembrance of Me." Could we possibly remember this great act of our salvation "too often"? I don't think so.

Jesus said, "as often as you eat this bread and drink this cup, you proclaim the Lord's death until He comes".

I, for one, am happy to know that a Sunday will never pass in the future of this congregation when the Christ's death will not be remembered and proclaimed around this table.

NOT IN CIRCLES

(42) Two children took all their money and rode a merry-go-round until their money was all gone. They had gone around and around for quite a long time. Their mother spoke briefly to then, "Well — I see you finally got off. I just want to know one thing, where have you been?"

Communion should not be just a matter of going in circles for the Christian. It is indeed the same experience — but we should be changing — growing each time we gather again with Christ, to remember Him.

IT WASN'T EASY

(43) It isn't easy to be in Church every Sunday morning. It isn't easy to take an active and responsible part in the life of the church.

It isn't easy to teach a class, or call on the lost, or develop your talents.

It isn't easy to love when you aren't loved, or forgive when you aren't forgiven. It isn't easy to guide your mind along the thoughts that are fitting for the Lord's Supper.

In fact, it isn't easy to be a Christian!

But then — it wasn't easy to die on a cross — was it?

MY SIN

(44) My God! My God! And can it be
That I should sin so lightly now,
And think no more of evil thoughts
Than of the wind that waves the bough?

Ever when tempted, make me see,

Beneath the Olives' noon-pierced shades,
My Lord, alone, outstretched, and bruised,
And bleeding on the earth He made!

And make me feel it was my sin,
As though no other sins there were,
That was to Him, who bears the world,
A load that He could scarcely bear.

(Author Unknown)

LOYALTY TEST

(45) The Lord's Supper is a test of loyalty! What could be more simple or beautiful than this remembrance of Him. We need this weekly test. It is our soul meter. If we find that we have grown indifferent to this opportunity to gather at the Lord's Table, it is time for us to be alarmed about our spiritual life.

For Special Sundays

UNCERTAINTY OF LORD'S SUPPER

(46) The Lord's Supper is like March. We are a little uncertain about the weather. We don't know whether to really enjoy these beautiful days, for fear that more bad weather is on the way.

We are also a little uncertain about this meeting with Christ at His table. We are a little afraid that coming face to face with our sin and its effect on Christ may be a burden — greater than the blessing of being reminded of His forgiveness of all our sins.

Let's remember — in Christ, the blessing is always more permanent than the burden.

WORLD COMMUNION

(47) "...We, who are many, are one body in Christ, and individually members one of another..." (Romans 12:5, NASV).

Union with the Lord Jesus Christ also involves mutual union with other members of the body. We are united not only with His body, but with the church also. The church lives and moves in our community and throughout the world. This fact should speak to us about our relationship with other persons. It condemns us if that relationship is bad. We are one body in Christ.

THANKSGIVING

(48) The story is told that when Kipling was one of the most popular writers of his day he received ten shillings for every word he wrote. Someone sent him ten shillings and asked that he send "one of your very best words". Kipling cabled back: "Thanks!"

This is a marvelous word. It means a great deal to both hearer and speaker. We are filled with thankfulness as we gather about this table. The person who cannot be thankful has removed such a blessing from his life.

We gather here today not only to remember but to give THANKS.

CHRISTMAS

(49) A small boy looking at a picture of his absent father, told his mother, "I wish Father would just step out of this picture."

We all are like that with God. Ideas and pictures leave something more to be desired. They are not enough. We want personal contact.

This is what happened. God, the Father, in the person of His Son, stepped out of the picture of heaven into human life. "And the Word became flesh..." (John 1:14, NASV).

This is the meaning of Christmas. Phillips Brooks said "Christmas once — is Christmas still!" To think of His death is to remember His birth and the reason for His coming.

CHRISTMAS

(50) "He who has not Christmas in his heart will never find it under a tree." — Roy L. Smith.

The same is true concerning Communion. This is not where we meet Christ for the first time. This is the renewing of a previous relationship. That's why it is a meaningless experience for the person who is not acquainted with Christ!

CHRISTMAS

(51) We approach the stable of Bethlehem and we can see a rough hewn cradle, made of wood, padded by straw, and pressed into place by 6 or 7 pounds of struggling humanity. But we see more than just a beautiful baby as we come to this table.

We see a fully grown man...

    suffering...
      dying...
        giving...
          forgiving...
            dying...
              loving...
                promising...
                  dying...

EASTER

(52) His body — broken! Killed! Cut by nails and spears. His blood flowing from punctured wounds covering ... a heart that — beats... no more! But from our thankful remembering — the Easter message brings us cause to rejoice.

Death could not hold Him.

A dead God — not dead!

Gary G. Jenkins is a
Christian Church minister
who was born in Wichita,
Kansas. He received his
education from Milligan
College and Emmanuel
School of Religion in
Eastern Tennessee. Gary
G. Jenkins served in the
ministry for 41 years in
Tennessee, Ohio,
Pennsylvania, Illinois
and Oklahoma. He and his
wife, Janet, have two
grown children
and five grandchildren.
Gary is semi-retired (see
Numbers 8:24-26) in
Oklahoma. He is the
author of another book,
It Really Happened
That Way.

Made in the USA
Middletown, DE
03 September 2023

37878757R00018